T0063921

IMAGE BOOSTER

CLAUDETTE FRANCIS

AuthorHouse™
1663 Liberty Drive
Bloomington, IN 47403
www.authorhouse.com
Phone: 1-800-839-8640

Published by AuthorHouse 10/15/2014

ISBN: 978-1-4969-4615-7 (sc)
ISBN: 978-1-4969-4614-0 (e)

Contents

ALSO BY CLAUDETTE FRANCIS

The Mystery of the Resurrection
An Inspirational Drama on the Resurrection of Jesus Christ
...with Testimonies from High-Profile Star Witnesses

Jesus Is Risen
An Easter Play for Children

The Mystery of the Nativity
An Inspirational Drama on the Nativity of Jesus Christ
...with Testimonies from High-Profile Star Witnesses

Study Guide and Workbook to Accompany the Mystery of the Nativity

Children's Bible Stories Workbook
Stories from the New Testament

Student Testimonials

I am happy when you talk about Jesus because it teaches me something more about God, Jesus, and me. You help me realize my value more.

You know exactly what to say to encourage us to be what we want to be when we grow up.

When I finally find the career I would like to work in, I should not let anyone discourage me from developing it.

I like how you talk about God—and how we should never be afraid to do what God is calling us to do.

I never had so much confidence in God until I heard your messages.

You made me realize that God is all around us—and that he loves us very much.

You encouraged me to start reading the Bible. You can ask my brother. We are both reading the Bible now.

I wish you could tell us more about God. No one ever told us so much about God. I told my friends that you are always talking about God.

Are you going to tell us more messages about God tomorrow?

I enjoy listening to you speak about God.

I really like how you talk about yourself and God. It gives me a lot of confidence.

Please write your messages in a book—and go tell the high school kids about them. I have a brother in high school, and he needs to hear these messages.

Introduction

This book was inspired by the real-life experiences of the author, who taught in elementary schools in Guyana and Canada.

After decades of teaching, Francis developed her own style of dealing with her young charges. The young people of her day obeyed their parents, their teachers, and others in authority because they were afraid of the punishment that would follow if they disobeyed. Since they did not want to endure the pain, they complied in a docile, passive manner—even if their inner rebellious minds did not want to do so.

Today's young people, in contrast, do not respond very well to fear; they appear to respond better to love. The concept of love makes them trust and obey more willingly. Francis believes that where there is love, there is also God, and where God is, fear slowly dissipates. The Bible says that God did not give us the spirit of fear, rather the spirit of power, love, and self-discipline (2 Timothy 1:7).

The young people loved her messages and stories and wanted to hear them repeatedly. Francis' aim was always to empower students to know God, love God, and serve God and their neighbours. She always encouraged the young people to ask God for wisdom, understanding, and knowledge—three basic gifts they need to navigate this complex world.

These messages certainly provide a sound basis for their future explorations in the Holy Scriptures because students have gone to the Bible to find out for themselves what the Bible has to say.

What a tremendous difference these messages have made in the lives of young people! They perceive themselves as better human beings, and they are more confident and more at peace with themselves and their neighbours. It was precisely because of the reaction to the messages that Francis was inspired to title this book *Image Booster.*

It has been Francis' experience that even very young people show a deep hunger for the Word of God. In this respect, Francis believes that she is delivering to the young people what they want. She certainly makes a connection with them, and she gives them the tools they need to go out and meet life's challenges with courage and hope. Although these messages are written for young people, Francis is confident that adults will also find them educational, instructional, and inspirational.

To God be the glory, praise, honour, and thanksgiving.

Be Grateful for Today

It is good to give thanks to the Lord,
To sing praises to your name, O Most High;
To declare your steadfast love in the morning,
And your faithfulness by night.
—Psalm 92:1–2

We thank you, God, for giving us a fresh new day. How good it is to be alive today? When I get out of bed in the mornings, I go to my window, look at the fresh new day, take in a deep breath, then lift up my hands in praise to God, and say, "Thank you, God, for your gift of this new day. Give me the grace to spend it wisely."

Look through your own windows now to behold this fresh, new day! Lovely, isn't it? Today is a gift from God. We did not have this day yesterday, and we certainly will not have it tomorrow. How about that?

Quietly thank God for today. How do you react when you receive a gift from a family member or a friend? You jump up and down and thank the person. You might even give the person a big hug or a kiss.

You open your gift, and your face lights up with joy. You show your gift to all those around you. You think, *I will cherish this for the rest of my life.*

It is the same with this gift of a new day from God. Now that you have this new day, what are you going to do with it? Please allow me to make some suggestions.

Be a better person than you were yesterday.
Be more caring.
Help someone you have never helped before.
Be more attentive.
Spend more time reading, studying, learning,
and praying.
Be more respectful to family members. Tell them
you love them with acts of kindness. Show them
how much you love them.

Are there people who really get on your nerves? Show them kindness—and pray for them today.

If you are accustomed to using bad words, make an effort today to clean up your speech. If you know that you are inclined to bully others, let today be the day you stop that.

Be kind to one another, be tender hearted, and forgive one another. Be imitators of God, as beloved children, and live in love, as Christ loved us and gave himself up for us (Ephesians 4:32, 5:1–2).

Share something with the poor today. It could be money, food, clothes, kind words, or a prayer. I am sure we can all add many more suggestions to this list. Who is bold enough to add one more suggestion to this list? Don't be shy. There are so many things we can do today to show our gratitude to God for giving us another new day. At the end of the day, we can say that we spent our twenty-four hours wisely. Bravo!

This day has a date assigned to it. What is today's date? Say it out loudly. Let us not mix up day with date.

A day can be Monday, Tuesday, Wednesday, Thursday, Friday, Saturday, or Sunday, but a date is a month, day, and year. Now consider this. If you live to be sixty, seventy, eighty, or even a hundred years old, you will never see this date again. Today's date will be with us until midnight, and then it will be gone forever—never to return. When you wake up tomorrow morning, you will be looking at a new date.

Many persons did not see this new day. Sickness, disease, accidents, famine, natural disasters, and other unfortunate circumstances ended their journeys yesterday. I look at my days on this earth as a journey. I am on a journey back to God. Jesus came to this earth, journeyed here, and then went back to heaven.

You are on that same journey. Earth is not your destination. One day you will meet God. Those persons who did not see this new day ended their journeys yesterday. We, on the other hand, have been given another day on our journey. Spend it wisely!

Here is an opportunity to embrace this fresh, new day and live it to its fullest. Be grateful for today. Make it your best day ever. God promises to help you.

The Bible says, "Blessed be the Lord who daily bears us up" (Psalm 68:19).

We have all the help we need. Let's show the Lord how grateful we are for today. Do not miss any opportunity to do good for your brothers and sisters in Christ.

Prayer

Thank you, God, for your gift of this new day. I want to be a much better person than I was yesterday. Bless me with wisdom, strength, understanding, courage, and knowledge to live this new day to its fullest. Amen.

Bless You

God spoke a blessing over Adam and Eve.
God blessed them, and God said to
them, "Be fruitful and multiply,
And fill the earth and subdue it, and have
dominion over the fish of the sea
And over the birds of the air, and
over every living thing
That moves upon the earth."
—Genesis 1:28

You are everything to me, Lord. Whatever I am today, you made it possible. Help me to fulfill my God-given potential. Give me the grace to empower others as I say blessings over them. A blessing is something powerful—if it is done the right way. Usually we wait for someone to sneeze before we say, "Bless you." Is that all there is to a blessing? Certainly not!

God spoke a blessing over the first people. Listen to the blessing. Scripture says that God blessed them.

Be fruitful and multiply, and fill the earth and subdue it, and have dominion over the fish of the sea and over the birds of the air and over every living thing that moves upon the earth. See, I have given you every plant-yielding seed that is upon the face of all the earth, and every tree with the seed in its fruit; you shall have

them for food. And to every beast of the earth,
and to every bird of the air, and to everything
that creeps on the earth, everything that has the
breath of life, I have given every green plant for
food. (Genesis 1:28–30).

How did God bless the first humans? First of all, he
spoke words to them. Secondly, he did not wait for them
to sneeze before saying, "Bless you!" He told them what
was in the blessing. He empowered them by giving
them the power and the ability to have dominion and
rule over all that he created. It was a great responsibility,
but God blessed them with the ability to do it.

To bless someone, you have to empower the person
by speaking special words over them. You have to
enable the person to achieve something. Just saying,
"Bless you!" when a person sneezes does not empower
them to do anything.

Speaking words of blessings should become such a
habit in you that every day you would speak blessings to
your mom, dad, brothers, sisters, other family members,
friends, teachers, and even your enemies.

Bless them with words that do them good. When you
bless them, you should speak words to empower them,
make them feel that they can achieve great things, and
make them challenge themselves to do the impossible.

The Bible tells us about blessing being significant.
Fathers spoke the blessing over their children. As a
matter of fact, the children wanted to hear the blessings
before their father died. Abraham, Isaac, and Jacob

spoke the blessing over their children. They let their children know what to expect in their lives. Would you like to hear others speak blessings over you? I think so.

What is the opposite of *bless*? The opposite of bless is *curse*. Nobody wants to hear a curse spoken over his or her life? Yet many people do just that.

Sometimes parents speak curses over their own children, friends speak curses over their friends, or families speak curses over members of their own families. Is that what God wants us to do? Certainly not! God wants us to speak blessings over one another. Speak something beautiful — even over our enemies.

You may think it is not fair to bless those who persecute you, pick on you, or bully you. That's really hard, but once we begin practicing it, it will become easier.

Jesus said, "Love your enemies. Do good to those who hate you. Bless those who curse you. Pray for those who abuse you" (Luke 6:27:28). What would you say to Jesus? "Give me a break, Jesus? Do you really expect me to follow your advice?"

If Jesus tells you to do something, he will give you the grace to do it; in other words, it means that it is possible to be done. Imagine blessing bullies, speaking kind words over them, or praying for them, and seeing their lives turn around. That would be awesome, wouldn't it? Someday they might return to you and thank you for blessing them instead of cursing them and hating them because the blessing you spoke over their lives was so powerful. It changed them, and now they are grateful to you.

A student once complained that another student had hurt her feelings badly. She asked me what she should do.

I replied, "Pray for that student."

The next morning, the student returned to me and said, "Teacher, it worked!"

I asked, "What worked?"

With a big smile, she said, "I prayed for my enemy last night, and today we are best friends again."

I replied, "Congratulations! Go and spread the good news!"

Pray for one another. Speak blessings—and not curses. Do not wait for someone to sneeze before saying, "Bless you!"

Here are some blessings you can speak over the lives of friends:

> *God bless you with courage, boldness, and good success in your schoolwork.*
> *God bless you with the ability to fulfill your dreams for your life.*

Here is a blessing you can speak over the lives of bullies:

> *God bless you with a kind and peaceful heart so that you can do good—and not harm—to your brothers and sisters in Christ.*

Here are some blessings you can speak over the life of your mother:

> *God bless you and make you the very best mom*
> *in the whole world.*
> *God bless you with good health, joy, and peace.*

Here is a blessing you can speak over the life of your father:

> *God bless you and make you strong, healthy, and courageous—and may God grant you a successful day!*

Here is a blessing you can speak over the life of your teacher:

> *God bless you with his love and grace. May your day be fruitful, successful, and happy in this classroom! May you have the cooperation of your students all day long!*

These blessings build persons up instead of tearing them down. Learn to say blessings that are meaningful. Do you know that you can speak blessings over yourself too? Try this! Say your name and then say, "Bless me, God, with the courage to become the person you called me to be! Bless me with beauty, wisdom, riches, and success. Bless me with boldness and courage so that I can make the world a better place."

Speak a blessing over someone today. If you continually bless others, they may do the same for you. Before long, we will have a blessed community.

May God bless you! May he empower you to be strong and courageous today!

Prayer

Father God, empower me to be the kind of person you intended me to be. I know that you want me to show others how much you care for me by the way you bless me. Make me a blessing so that I can bless others. Amen.

Christ's Ambassador

Jesus said, "Go into all the world and proclaim
the good news to the whole creation."
—Mark 16:15

Who has ever met an ambassador? Let's just imagine that you are grown up and working in a government office. You get a call from a government official who elevates you from your present position to an ambassador. What would you do? To help you understand what this means, we first have to find out who is an ambassador—and what an ambassador does.

An ambassador is a person who is sent to another country to live and work there. An ambassador represents his or her home country and deals with the country's interests as well as the interests of the international community.

Now that you know who an ambassador is and what an ambassador's job is, you can begin to appreciate the role of an ambassador. I want to talk about a *heavenly* ambassador. A heavenly ambassador is an ambassador for Jesus and his kingdom.

Imagine yourself as a heavenly ambassador. You are coming to earth to represent Jesus and his kingdom. Where will you start? You will have to start by talking about the things of heaven. Therefore, you have to be very knowledgeable about the kingdom of heaven and what Jesus taught about the kingdom. To whom are you going to talk? Obviously you will be talking to the heads of nations on earth.

Before you can be accepted for that position by the heads of the nations, you will have to show them your credentials. What are credentials? Credentials are important documents—papers, identity cards, passports, certificates, or references—that prove you are who you say you are and that you are qualified to represent your country, which is heaven.

As an ambassador, what would you take on your journey? A Bible, charts, maps, and clothing. You will have to say good-bye to all your friends in heaven since you will be on a journey that could take at least five years. You are heading to earth to be an ambassador for Jesus and heaven. You are going to a place that is two-thirds water and one-third land. You will see people of many races, colours, and sizes. Can you tell them about the good news of heaven? Are you qualified to relate Jesus' teachings? Can you tell them who God is? Can you tell them what heaven is like? Can you tell them why Jesus came to this earth? He was very happy in heaven, but he left heaven and came to earth. What was his purpose in doing so? Can you tell them what the Ten Commandments are? Can you tell them about Jesus' New Rule of Love?

What is the New Rule of Love? Can you explain terms like repentance, discrimination, forgiveness, justice, peace, and happiness? What do you think about family, friends, and enemies? Did Jesus teach about bullying, drugs, alcohol, and swearing? Can you give advice on any of these?

Jesus is in heaven now, but he is coming back to earth. No one knows when except God. In the meantime, while we are awaiting his return, we can busy ourselves with helping others to know, love, and serve him in this world. Who is ready and willing to accept the job?

I do not want to leave all of the young, willing, and faithful ambassadors for the kingdom of heaven with the impression that being an ambassador is without dangers, difficulties, threats, and disappointments. You have to be prepared for these things.

Jesus, Peter, Paul, James, and others had very great challenges, sufferings, and disappointments as they proclaimed the good news. Please do not think you will escape suffering and persecution. As an ambassador, you will face discouragement. You will be inclined to quit out of fear of what is happening to you. But hold on and finish your mission. You will be able to draw strength from Jesus because he suffered throughout his ministry.

Prayer

Jesus my Lord, I want to represent you on the earth. Give me the grace to be faithful to your teaching and to proclaim the good news to the whole creation. Give me the grace to endure when the going gets rough. Amen.

Cut Off

How can young people keep their way pure?
By guarding it according to your Word.
With my heart, I seek you;
Do not let me stray from your commandments.
I treasure your Word in my heart,
So that I may not sin against you.
Blessed are you, O Lord; teach me your statutes.
—Psalm 119:9–12

Have you ever been speaking on the telephone when suddenly there is silence? You say, "My phone is dead! What happened?"

Did your phone really die? Of course not! The phone was cut off from its power source. Maybe someone unplugged it by accident or there was a blackout. In the same way we can experience that kind of death, we can feel cut off from God. He is our source.

We cut ourselves off from God when we engage in wrongdoing. Do not be discouraged. There is hope for each of us. When we commit wrong acts, we should not hide ourselves like Adam and Eve did in the Garden of Eden. We do not have to cut ourselves off from God. Instead of hiding from God, we should run to God. He is gracious and merciful enough to forgive us.

What really surprises me is the number of young people who really feel that God stopped loving them because of something they did wrong. They want to apologize, but they cannot because they feel cut off from God. They do not think that saying sorry is enough to make God forgive them. They carry this great weight of guilt upon their shoulders and become grumpy.

Young people often ask, "Do you think God still loves me after what I did?"

I always say, "Yes, of course God still loves you after what you did. You cannot make God not love you. God is love!"

God loves you because of what Jesus did. Jesus suffered and died on the Cross and paid the penalty for our sins. In other words, Jesus died so that we might live.

Jesus went to dinner at Matthew's house. Matthew was a tax collector who was hated by his friends. His job allowed him to collect taxes from the people and hand it over to the government. However, he also took extra money from the people and kept it for himself. That was not fair; he was very dishonest. Because of his bad reputation, he was looked upon as a big sinner. The people shunned him, and they would have nothing to do with him. The other tax collectors were treated in the same manner because they too were unfair and dishonest.

Jesus went to eat with a big sinner and many other sinners. When the Pharisees—religious men—saw this, they said to Jesus' disciples, "Why does your teacher eat with tax collectors and sinners?"

I love Jesus' reply.

Jesus said, "I have come to call not the righteous but sinners." You can read Jesus's entire reply in (Matthew 9:9–13).

God loves the sinners—not their sins. He loves them unconditionally, fully, and completely. God does not ask us to do anything for him before he can love us. He loves us regardless of whether we love him or not. Performing great works and making big sacrifices for God will not make God love us more or less.

Whether we are good or bad, he already loves us with an everlasting love. We are his children, and he loves us. He cares for us. He sent his Son to die for our sins so we do not have to die for our sins. We do not have to cut ourselves off from such a loving God. Thank God for that—that is how much he loves you and me. Once you understand God's unconditional love, you will not want to do anything to offend him. You will keep his commandments out of love for him.

Because God loves us so much, we want to show him how much we love him too. We try our best to please him. If we sin or do wrong things, we should repent and move on with our lives. God does not want the persons who commit sins to die; he wants them to turn from their sins and live.

Stop being grumpy! Move on with your life. Understand that none of us is perfect. We can all practice doing what is right, and that will eventually help us reach our goal of perfection.

Prayer

Lord God, give me the grace to remain in your friendship always. I am sorry for anything wrong I did in the past. Please forgive me. I will try to do better from this day forward. Thank you for sending your Son Jesus to die for me on the Cross and pay the price for my sins. Amen.

Do You Play the Blame Game?

God said to Adam, "Have you eaten from the
tree of which I commanded you not to eat?"
The man said, "The woman whom you gave to be
with me, she gave me fruit from the tree, and I ate."
—Genesis 3:11–12

A teacher calls out, "Joe, where is your homework?"

Joe answers, "Sorry, Miss Brown. The dog ate my homework."

Another teacher calls out, "Ann, where is your homework?"

Ann answers, "Sorry, Mr. Harding. My baby brother puked all over my homework, and I had to throw it out."

How many of you know that the two kids were playing the Blame Game? The rule of this game is that the players must make somebody or something else take the blame for their mistakes. Do you know kids who are very good at this game? Perhaps you emerge the winner every time.

Let's find out how this game started and who the first players were. For the answer, we will have to go all the way back to the beginning of the book of Genesis the first book in the Bible.

According to the story, God said to Adam, "You may freely eat of every tree in the garden, but of the fruit from the tree of the knowledge of good and evil, you shall not eat, for in the day that you eat of it, you shall die (Genesis 2:16–17).

Adam disobeyed God and ate the fruit. When God asked him why he ate the fruit, he played the first ever Blame Game. Adam blamed his wife. He said, "The woman whom you gave me to be with me, she gave me fruit from the tree, and I ate" (Genesis 3:12).

When it was Eve's turn to play the Blame Game, she blamed the serpent. She said, "The serpent tricked me, and I ate" (Genesis 3:13).

All of you must have played the Blame Game at one time or another in your lives. It is the oldest game in the history of humanity. Anyone—old or young—can play it. I am quite sure that I play the Blame Game as well. We still blame the serpent, our parents, our teachers, our friends, and our neighbours. We blame everybody and everything for our faults. We even blame God when things go wrong. It seems that we are born with the ability to blame someone or something.

What is the opposite of blame? It is taking responsibility for our actions. To own up! If you are constantly playing the Blame Game, then you can change that habit today. By accepting responsibility for your own wrongdoing, you can rid yourself of this bad habit. When you are accused of doing something wrong and you know you did it, own up to it. Say, "I did it, and I am sorry." These are seven of the hardest words to say, but they can get you out of a whole lot of trouble. Practice does make perfect.

Prayer

Jesus, teach me to have the courage to speak the truth always—even if it hurts. Grant me the grace to take responsibility for my faults and to not place the blame on others. Amen.

Fear Not

For God did not give us a spirit of cowardice (fear),
But rather a spirit of power and of
love and of self-discipline.
—2 Timothy 1:7

Have you ever counted the number of times the word
fear appears in the Bible? There are sixty-six books in
the Bible,[1] and the word *fear* appears in fifty-two of
them. The word *fear* appears more than one hundred
times in the Bible. Over and over, it says, "Fear not."
At other times, we read, "Do not be afraid," yet we are
very fearful.

Even the shepherds were afraid on that first
Christmas night when an angel of the Lord stood before
them. They were terrified when they saw the angel. The
angel had to help them get rid of their fear. The angel
said, "Do not be afraid; for I am bringing you good
news of great joy for all the people" (Luke 2:9–10).

If you say you have no fear, you would not be telling
the truth. All of us have fear, and we show we have
fear many times during the day. Do you know that
our pets and other animals also have fear? Fear is an
emotion that human beings and animals possess. Our

---

1   Mears, C. Henrietta, *What the Bible Is All About*, Bible
    Handbook, NIV Edition, Regal, California, 1998, p. 11.

dog becomes extremely fearful when he hears thunder, and he trembles uncontrollably. Marty runs and hides in closets, under the bed, in the bathtub, or anyplace where he feels safe. He believes the thunder cannot reach him there. Even when we call him by name, he refuses to leave his hiding place. He is too afraid to come out to eat his favourite food; he hides himself until the thunder ceases.

It is true that not all fear is bad; there are times when fear is good. It is a signal that warns us to be careful so we don't suffer the consequences of our carelessness. No one would say, "I have no fear of the traffic!" and walk straight into oncoming traffic. They would wait on the sidewalk for the traffic to pass and look to the right, to the left, then right again. If there were no approaching traffic, they would cautiously cross the street. That would be the right thing to do!

Most of the time, fear is useless. We fear things that may not even happen. We fear falling, but we never fall. We fear snakes, but we never see any snakes. We fear spiders, but they never come near us. We are afraid of airplanes, sickness, mice, dogs, grasshoppers, and bullies. The list goes on and on. What are some of your greatest fears?

Everyone feels fear at one time or another, but you do not have to let fear dominate your life. Don't let it stop you from doing what you have to do or from becoming what God wants you to become.

God wants us free of all those fears. Be strengthened today. Be courageous—and don't be afraid! Be free from all fears, jealousy, bullying, unforgiving spirits, selfishness, laziness, and all that you are afraid of. Get rid of fear and put on love instead.

Some of us suffer from excessive fear. Excessive fear is called phobia. Phobia is fear that has gotten out of control. It is fear that does not even make sense (e.g., you are in an elevator and you are so scared, so very, very afraid that the doors will not open when they should, that you want to jump out of the elevator. But since you can't, you cry or you perspire or you throw a tantrum from the panic you feel).

What is your greatest phobia? Are you really scared of being alone? Are you really scared of heights? Are you really scared of being locked in a cupboard? Are you really scared of snakes? Are you really scared of churches?

On one occasion, I invited a young person to pay a visit in a church.

The person answered, "Not me. I am very scared of going in there. It is dark and empty in there!" I replied, "What is there to be scared of? I believe that Jesus is in there, so I visit him whenever the opportunity arises."

I was puzzled at that young person's admission of the fear of visiting a church.

If you suffer from any form of fear, get closer to God. You have the greatest power on earth living inside you. You have God the Father, Son, and Holy Spirit to help you conquer any fear inside you. God will take away the fear, and he will replace it with his love and his power. He will give you a mind that is sound. You will be able to think things through sensibly.

"Be strong and courageous; do not be frightened or dismayed, for the Lord your God is with you wherever you go" (Joshua 1:9).

God is with you wherever you go. God is with you here and now. Cast your fears away. He cares for you. He will give you the grace to conquer your fears and phobias. However, I must caution you that you will have to be patient with yourself. You can get rid of your fears and phobias. You can do it! Yes, you can! I told you before that fear is an emotion, a feeling that all of us have. Some of us are more fearful than others. Some of us are fearful of one thing, and others have no fear of that thing at all.

After you have rid yourself of one fear, another fear may immediately take its place. Someone who was afraid of mice manages to get rid of that fear after listening to this message, but a fear of worms immediately replaces it. We have to be constantly on the lookout for fears of one kind or the other, and we must work to get rid of them when they overwhelm us.

In the Bible, we read about fear of the Lord. Does that mean that you have to be scared of God? No, this fear has another meaning. It means showing reverence toward God or being respectful to God. Use his name respectfully—and not as a curse word.

Prayer

Lord, your Word says that you did not give us a spirit of fear, but of power and love and a sound mind (2 Timothy 1–7). Please help me get rid of all useless fears so I can become courageous and bold for the sake of your kingdom. Amen.

Image Booster

So if anyone is in Christ, there is a new creation:
Everything old has passed away;
See, everything has become new!
—2 Corinthians 5:17

Change is one of the main ingredients of living life at its fullest. People should never say, "This situation cannot change because this is how it always was. It is too hard for me to change. This is the way I am."

This is a deception. It is not true. Things need to change; you need to change too. Change is the essence of growth. Not to change is not to live. Not to change is death! Just look at how much change has gone on in you since you were a baby. Many changes took place. You changed your size, your shape, your attitude, your personality, your voice, your friends, the way you dress, the way you talk, and the way you walk. Look at you now!

It is not fair to say you cannot change because that is the way you have always been. Change goes on daily—whether you notice it or not—and if you are honest with yourself, you can tell that you are constantly being changed. You are constantly creating a new image. In other words, you are constantly giving yourself a makeover. You are creating a new you. Celebrate that!

I welcome change into my life. As a matter of fact, I pursue it on a daily basis. My philosophy is to learn something new every day, and that something new must be capable of bringing about some positive change in my life. Before you lie down to sleep at night, ask yourself these two questions, "Did I learn something new today? How did it change my life for the better?"

Change must, first of all, come from within ourselves. Changing ourselves will ultimately change those around us. The word change is a small, one-syllable word, but it is a very powerful word. Ask yourself, "What kind of change can affect my life today and affect the lives of those around me? Can I be more patient? Can I be more considerate? Can I be more loving? Can I show more kindness to others?"

When persons see these new changes in you, they can follow in your footsteps and create a new image for themselves too. Pursue change. Do not be satisfied to carry on in the same old way day after day, especially when that old way is not making you a better person.

While you are on the journey of change, you must be prepared to adapt to what is going on in your life at that moment. If what is going on is not to your liking, you have the obligation to change it. When you wake up, look in the mirror. If you do not like what you see, make some changes. Create a new image. This is your challenge from this day on!

If you look in the mirror and like what you see, you probably have a good self- image. You are confident. You can make things happen. You feel good about yourself. You feel like you are on top of the world. You go out into your community and feel like shaking hands with everyone you meet. You say, "Good morning. How are you today?"

On the other hand, if you do not like what you see, you probably do not have a good self- image. You feel down. You feel like everyone is going to be against you. You feel like going back to bed because you know that it is not your day. You feel a headache coming on. What can you do? You need an image booster! You can change that poor image of yourself. You can create a new you. You have the power to do it! You have the ability to do just that!

Go to your closet and choose a pretty, brightly coloured outfit for the day. Smile at yourself. Hum a song, eat your breakfast, and go out there to face the world. Even if you do not feel like it, shake other students' hands and say, "Good morning. How are you?"

Try it and you will be surprised at how you have created a new you for yourself. Get excited about change! Don't try to be the same you as yesterday. Put on a new image—a brand-new you—today! Do you know that your image will determine how others see you and treat you? I often hear students say, "But so-and-so does not like me." I wonder what sort of image those students are showing to others. Is it a friendly image or a mean image?

Remember:

If you want to have friends, you have to be a friend first.

*If you want to be respected, you have to show
respect first.*

*If you want others to be patient with you, you
have to show patience first.*

*If you want to have joy in your life, you have to
give joy first.*

*If you want others to love you, you have to show
love first.*

If you want to receive, you have to give first.

Embrace change, renew your mind, and create a bright future for yourself and others. You have God's assurance of a new you.

Apostle Paul wrote, "So if anyone is in Christ, there is a new creation: everything old has passed away" (2 Corinthians 5:17). See? Everything has become new.

Clap your hands. Get excited! Jump up! Welcome the new you. By virtue of your baptism, you are in Christ. God has given you many gifts that you can work with to continue creating that new you. The best gift God has given you is the gift of love. With love in your heart, you can go out and change others. Become an image booster!

Prayer

Help me, dear Lord, to make necessary changes in my life. I want to become the person you want me to be. Amen.

Live the God Kind of Love

Love is patient; love is kind; love is not envious
or boastful or arrogant or rude.
It does not insist on its own way; it is not irritable
or resentful;
It does not rejoice in wrongdoing, but rejoices
in the truth.
It bears all things, believes all things, hopes all
things, and endures all things.
Love never ends.
—1 Corinthians 13:4–7

God's love for us is steadfast. It does not change. It is
faithful, reliable, loyal, steady, and true. We cannot stop
God from loving us.

Human love, on the other hand, is sometimes
unfaithful, unreliable, disloyal, unsteady, and untrue.
It acts according to emotions. It is like some of our other
emotions, such as fear or anger. Emotions are feelings
on the inside of us. They keep changing, according
to our moods. Today we feel mad, and tomorrow we
feel glad. Today we feel angry, and tomorrow we feel
happy. Today we feel love, and tomorrow we feel hate.
Today we feel happy, and tomorrow we feel sad. How
many times have you heard someone say, "Control your
emotions"? It is easy for them to say so, but it is not
always easy for us to control our emotions.

God's love does not go through the same kind of rollercoaster emotions as people's love does. Today we are loved, and tomorrow we are hated because of something we did wrong. We can be sure of God's love for us. He loves us very much today, and he will love us very much tomorrow. You can be sure of that.

God's love for us is unconditional. What is unconditional? It is doing something without expecting something in return. In most cases, people want us to do something to get their love. We say people's love has strings attached. They only love you when you do something for them. That's not what God expects of us. I help my friend clean up the mess because I want to—and because I love my friend. I am not expecting him to give me his lunch because I helped him clean up the mess. You do not have to do something for God so he will love you. He loves you because you are his child.

Jesus said, "Love your enemies and pray for those who persecute you (Matthew 5:44), that is the kind of love that God expects of us. When you do these things, you may be called crazy or foolish or stupid, but do them anyway. This is divine love—the God kind of love. Emulate it! This kind of divine love goes against human love.

Jesus told us to love even our enemies. He said, "If you love those who love you, what reward do you have?" (Matthew 5:46). Think about this!

If you want love, give love.
If you want friends, be a friend.

If you want respect, show respect.
If you want money, give away money.
If you want compassion, show compassion.
If you want mercy, show mercy.

Follow Jesus' example of love, and live the kind of love that he has for us. Jesus went throughout Galilee, teaching in their synagogues and proclaiming the good news of the kingdom and curing every disease and every sickness among the people (Matthew 4:23).

Continue to be good to others without always expecting good to be done to you in return. Jesus, who is God as well as man, said, "I give you a new commandment—that you love one another. Just as I have loved you, you also should love one another. By this, everyone will know that you are my disciples if you have love for one another. (John 13:34–35).

Ask yourself, "Am I obeying Jesus' new commandment? Do I love my friends just as Jesus loves me? If not, why not?"

Every day, there are many opportunities for you to show love for one another. Are you patient with the person who is a little slower than you are? Do you show kindness to the person who does not want to be your friend? That's a difficult one, isn't it? Do you forgive the persons who wrong you or make them pay for what they did to you?

Look beyond yourself, help somebody else, and resolve to follow in the footsteps of Jesus. Furthermore, practice the love of God every time an opportunity arises. In other words, observe the Golden Rule: "In everything, do to others as you would have them do to you; for this is the law and the prophets" (Matthew 7:12).

Prayer

"For the mountains may depart and the hills be removed, but my steadfast love shall not depart from you," says the Lord (Isaiah 54:10).

Living Memories

"For surely I know the plans I have
for you," says the Lord,
"Plans for your welfare and not for harm,
to give you a future with hope."
—Jeremiah 29:11

Growing up was not easy for me. Very early in life, I knew my gift was teaching. I studied hard, and my father made sure I kept studying hard. The most difficult part of my studies involved memorizing the multiplication tables: two times two up to twenty-five times twenty-five. It was boring and difficult for me, but by the time I was ten years old, I knew them all.

Some of the tables were easy, but others were very difficult to memorize. The worst were thirteen, nineteen, and twenty-three. These were very challenging, yet I had to recite them to my father every Sunday after I returned from participating in the church service. I started with two times one is two and ended with twenty-five times twenty-five is 625. Yes, I can still remember that.

When I grew up, I chose teaching as my career. I taught many children the art of learning. My students were eager to learn, and I was eager to provide the necessary support for their development.

My teaching experience started in my native land in September 1954. On July 20, 1969, I left my native land for Canada. That was a very memorable day for me. Something very special happened that day. I will excuse you if you do not know the answer because you were not yet born. On that beautiful Sunday, Neil Armstrong, Edwin Aldrin, and Michael Collins, American astronauts, landed on the moon. I was 35,000 feet up in the air when the pilot announced over the PA system that the men had landed on the moon. Spontaneous applause filled the cabin, and from that day on, I always associate my landing in Canada with the astronauts landing on the moon.

For those of you who were born outside of Canada, I guess that you too can associate some important thing that happened to you on the day you left your native country and landed in Canada.

The biggest shock I received when I came to Canada was the first snowfall. My native country is situated in the tropics, and I had heard about snow, but when I saw it for the first time, I was caught unaware. I didn't know what I was looking at through the window of the apartment where I was staying.

I actually thought that somebody's chimney was broken, and I was looking at the ashes being carried away by the wind. But as I continued peering through the window, I noticed the ashes were becoming more plentiful in the sky. I decided to go out on the balcony to better observe this phenomenon. I let some of the ash fall on my hand, and it felt cold. I asked myself if it was snow. Even though it was a rhetorical question, I answered in the affirmative. I was so thrilled that I stayed out there for a long time. I watched the flakes dancing through the sky and down to earth. I was mesmerized.

Cherish your own stories of wonder and glee. You may be sharing them with others someday.

Prayer

Lord, thank you for the beauty of life. Thank you for the wonderful experiences I continue to enjoy every day. Amen.

Love Letter to Jesus

My beloved is mine
And I am his.
—Song of Solomon 2:16

I wrote a personal love letter to my friend Jesus. Perhaps one day you too will write a similar love letter to your friend Jesus.

Dear loving Jesus,

Your words have been playing in my spirit for a long time, and now I have decided to let you know how I feel about you.

My sweet Lord, you said, "Come to me, all you that are weary and are carrying heavy burdens, and I will give you rest. Take my yoke upon you, and learn from me; for I am gentle and humble of heart, and you will find rest for your souls. For my yoke is easy, and my burden is light" (Matthew 11:28–30).

My dear Jesus, sometimes I get weary and tired, just as you got weary and tired and needed to rest. You would go away from the crowds and seek a lonely place in the desert or on a mountaintop or by the sea. One time, you were so tired you fell asleep on a pillow in a boat. I guess you would have come back refreshed, relaxed, rejuvenated, invigorated, and ready to continue with your Father's business.

Give me the courage to follow your example, my Lord Jesus. When I get weary and tired, help me find a lonely place where I can rest and be refreshed by you. Loving Lord, that place could be before you in the tabernacle in church or in the privacy of my room. Wherever that lonely place for me is, Lord, I am confident that I will find you there. You will be waiting to nourish me, anoint me, love me, comfort me, forgive me, care for me, and bind up and heal my wounds. Thank you, Lord, for this blessed assurance.

Dear loving Jesus, I thank you for being so near to me. Wherever I go, I will find you. I do not need to travel the world to find you. You are right here within me—in my spirit. Thank you, Lord. I need you now more than ever before. Satan, my enemy, knows what his future will be, and he is furious. He would like to devour all of your people, let him not devour me (1 Peter 5:8).

Lord Jesus, I am powerless to defeat him by myself, but I know in my heart that you are with me and will fight my battles for me. Please direct my path. Please give me the courage to fight with all my might. Help me fight temptations like you did. Help me fight fear, inferiority, forgetfulness, insecurity, stress, lack of forgiveness, hatred, doubt, disbelief, prejudice, temptations, and every other kind of pressure from within and without.

You promised never to leave me or forsake me. I receive that promise. I know that you are always there to help me. You love me so much that you laid down your life for me. Every time I think of what you did for me, I fall in love with you again. You are the most wonderful, the most awesome, and the sweetest person to ever come into my life. Until I see you face to face, I will cherish our precious moments together on earth.

Good-bye, my Jesus, my saviour, my God, my hero, my beloved, and my role model.

Your precious one,
    Claudette.

Prayer

I love you, Jesus, with my whole heart. Help me love you more and more each day. Amen.

Natural Gifts

Are all apostles? Are all prophets? Are all teachers? Do all work miracles?
Do all possess gifts of healing? Do all speak in tongues? Do all interpret?
But strive for the greater gifts, and I will show you a much more excellent way.
—1 Corinthians 12:29–31

Who gave us the universe? Who gave us his Son, Jesus? Who gave us this new day? All good gifts come from God. He gave us spiritual gifts, and he gave us natural gifts. Do you know you have a unique natural gift? Think about it!

God placed a gift inside of each one of us. Do you know what your gift is? Your gift can make you a success in life. Do you want to be a success? When you are considering your gift, there are three words you must think about. I refer to them as the Three Ds:

Discover: Find out what gift God gave you.
Develop: Take the time to study all you can about your gift.
Deploy: Use your gift to bring you success and help others.

What is your gift? Have you ever thought of your gift before? Some persons discover their gift when they are two, five, or seven. How old are you now? Twelve? That's a bit late, but do not worry. All is not lost.

Even though you may not have discovered your gift yet, you can certainly begin to think about it right now, and make plans to develop it.

Isn't it great to know that God never looks at color, race, or religion before bestowing a particular gift on a person? You can expect God to give you a gift that is unique and different from anybody else's.

After discovering and developing your gift, you must be resolved to deploy it. Deploy it means use it. Your gift is not for you alone—it is to be shared with others, just I am sharing my gift of teaching with you. I can see some of you becoming doctors, lawyers, teachers, priests, religious sisters, athletes, artists, astronauts, police officers, firemen, painters, construction workers, architects, presidents, and prime ministers. Can you see yourself as one of these? Well, then, so are you! From this day on, do what it takes to bring out that gift in you. Begin working on it now!

My gift is teaching. I entered the teaching profession as a teenager, and after twenty years, I decided that I had had enough of teaching. I wanted to change jobs and start a new career. I took some secretarial courses and hoped to begin my new career as an office secretary. When I could not find a job at the end of it all, I was very disappointed.

Suddenly, a teaching position became available and I was offered the job. I was wise enough to recognize that being an office secretary was not my gift from God.

My gift was teaching, and it was back to teaching for me. For many more years, I enjoyed my work teaching countless numbers of children. I taught until the time came for me to retire from the career I loved so much.

I attended retirement parties. I received gifts and letters from very important people. My retirement day was a very happy day for me. I awoke early in the morning and prepared my retirement speech.

The moment came for me to deliver the speech. Colleagues, friends, relatives, and family members all gathered in the hall, and I was having a very pleasant time. I started off fearlessly and boldly. Suddenly, I became sad and began to cry. Knowing I was going to leave behind a career that I had cherished so much for so long—knowing I was going to miss the daily routines of a classroom, the children, and my colleagues—overwhelmed me. Tears ran down my cheeks all the way through the rest of my speech. I did not expect to be so carried away by my emotions. It was heartrending to be on the stage, surrendering my God-given gift of teaching to go home to hang up my chalk and blackboard.

Fortunately, that was not the end of my story. Before I could begin to enjoy my retirement years, I was called back to work as a substitute teacher. Realizing that teaching was my gift, I accepted the position and taught for another five years before retiring a second time.

You might think that you need many gifts. Not true! One gift is enough. However, you must discover what that unique gift is. My gift has made me successful, and yours will do the same for you. When you discover what your gift is, set your mind to developing it. Work at it all the time. Imagine yourself doing it all day long. Become an expert at it. Keep practicing it. Keep pursuing it. Do not keep changing from one gift to another. Stick with it! You do not have to sell drugs. You do not have to wait for an inheritance. You do not have to steal or cheat. You can depend on your gift to make you prosperous. God is the one who gives you the ability to prosper, but you have to be faithful in pursuing your gift to the fullest.

What is your gift? To those of you who don't know, I say, "Ask your mom and dad, ask your teachers, or ask your friends. In many cases, your parents, teachers, and friends know what your gift is simply by observing you from day to day."

Over the years, many young people have shared their gifts with me: president, comedian, artist, pianist, computer programmer, architect, basketball player, soccer player, construction worker, doctor, dentist, teacher, Olympian, marine biologist, veterinarian, firefighter, police officer, chef, and lawyer.

If you already know what your gift is, you will not be drifting aimlessly through high school, or College or University. You will choose courses that will guide you in the right direction. You will not be wasting your time and thinking about dropping out. Therefore, your higher education school years will be most profitable. You will continue studying and preparing yourself for work in the real world. You will be working out your destiny.

I will be praying for you to discover and develop your individual gifts. Then you will certainly be in a position to use it to help yourself and others.

Prayer

May the gift you have bestowed on me, Lord, bring me success. Teach me to share its fruits with others. Amen.

No Time for God

He (Jesus) was praying in a certain place,
And after he had finished, one of his disciples
said to him,
"Lord, teach us to pray, as John taught his
disciples."
—Luke 11:1

From time to time, I hear students complain that
they can't find the time for prayers, God, and church.
Their defense is that they have too much to do. These
overwhelming tasks include homework, sports, and
housework.

Is it true? The following plan of action can help
students discover they do have time to spend with
prayer, God, and church. How wisely are you using
your daily twenty-four hours?

Work	8 hours
Sleep	8 hours
Eat and Drink	2 hours

Now that we have taken care of the most essential part
of our daily routine, let us calculate how many hours
they take. That is a total of eighteen hours. How many
hours are unaccounted for? Six hours. Let's add more
tasks to our daily routine.

Entertainment	2 hours
Grooming	½ *hour*
Hobbies	1 hour

The total is now 21½ *hours*. With that extra 2½ *hours, it is easy to see how you can certainly find time to spend with your God.*

Work (School)	8 hours
Sleep	8 hours
Meals	2 hours
Entertainment	2 hours
Grooming	½ *hour*
Hobbies	1 hour
Total hours spent	21½ hours

It is up to you to decide how much of that extra 2½ hours you can spend with God.

Many young people tell me that they have no time to pray, go to church, or take part in youth activities at the church. I hope that this exercise has convinced you that everyone can find half an hour per day to turn to God, church, and prayer. Prayer is having a conversation with God.

What a good habit to cultivate! Prayers do not have to be long; short prayers can be very effective. Here are some examples of short prayers:

My God I love you with my whole heart.
Help me, God. I am having difficulty with my work.

My dear Lord, my friend is not feeling well today. Please restore him/her to good health. Thank you, dear Jesus, for this very beautiful day. What a glorious sunrise we had this morning!

Prayer

Jesus, there are many times in the gospels when you went away to a secret place or the mountains to pray to your Heavenly Father. Teach me how to find precious moments during the day to speak with you. Amen.

Overcome Evil with Good

Be angry and do not sin,
Do not let the sun go down on your anger,
And do not make room for the devil.
—Ephesians 4:26–27

What do you think? Will a fireman try to put out a blazing fire with fire? Think about it! A fire is raging in the forest and burning up everything in its path. Flames are leaping heavenward, engulfing expensive houses and burning them to the ground. The fire is so intense that the firemen have to keep a distance.

If someone tells the firemen to douse the fire with more fire, what would you think of that person? You would certainly think that the person is crazy. So, too, you cannot fight evil with evil. The firemen have to use something much more calming than raging fire to extinguish the fire. We have to employ something much more calming than raging evil to extinguish evil. On one occasion, when the Samaritans did not receive Jesus into their village, the disciples James and John asked him if they could command fire from heaven to consume them, but Jesus turned and rebuked them (Luke 9:52-55).Every day, we encounter evil at home, in the schoolyard, on the streets, and almost anywhere people gather. How should we handle evil?

Imagine that someone is teasing you every day, perhaps saying evil things about you. Someone suggests throwing insults back at that person, but you know that it won't work. It would only spread and make the situation worse. You should try to fight that evil with love.

In the world, there is good and evil—just as we have long and short, black and white, old and young. Some people say, "If there is a God, why doesn't he remove all the evil from the world?" God will not do that because he gave us all free will. We can choose. We make our choices. We can choose to do evil or do good. Unfortunately, some persons choose to do evil.

Jesus told a parable about the wheat and the tares. The wheat represents good people, and the tares represent evil people. Tares were weeds that choke wheat. One day, a farmer sowed wheat in his field and went away. An enemy came along and sowed tares in the wheat field. When the wheat began to grow, the tares grew as well.

When the farmer returned, his workers asked, "Shall we pull up the tares?

The farmer said, "No, let them grow side by side until the harvest, because in digging up the tares, you will destroy the wheat. At harvest time, we will dig up the tares first and burn them in fire; afterward, we will gather the wheat and put it in the barns."

What is the point of this story? Jesus is saying that the good and the evil will live together, but the time will come when they will be separated.

Jesus experienced much evil while he was on earth, but he was able to overcome evil with good. What happened to him on the Cross was evil, yet he said, "Father, forgive them for they know not what they do."

Start challenging yourself to forgive others. You may get a passing grade on the way you handled the good that comes your way, but what sort of grade will you get for the way you treat the evil that comes your way? You'll have to strengthen your spirit. You will need God's grace to learn how to overcome evil with good.

God's ways are not our ways. Jesus said, "You have heard that it was said, you shall love your neighbour and hate your enemy. But I say to you, love your enemies and pray for those who persecute you so that you might be children of your Father in heaven, for he makes his sun rise on the evil and on the good, and he sends rain on the righteous and on the unrighteous" (Matthew 43–45).

It is comforting to know that God does not gather all the evil persons in one corner of the earth and say, "Okay, no sun for you. No rain for you!" His sun and his rain are for all his children—the good and the evil alike.

God does not want to get rid of the wicked. He wants them to turn away from their wicked ways. He gives them chance after chance to change their wicked ways and turn to him.

Prayer

Father, give me the grace to forgive those who hurt me by their wicked ways, as I forgive anyone I have hurt in any way. Amen.

Peer Pressure

The devil said to him (Jesus), "If
you are the Son of God,
Command this stone to become a loaf of bread."
Jesus answered him, "It is written, One
does not live by bread alone.'"
—Luke 4:3–4

Lola's friends stood around her and challenged her to walk across a big heap of stones without falling down. "Go, Lola, go! Go, Lola, go! Come on, Lola. You can do it! Walk, walk, walk!"

What do you think? Did she give in to the pressure that was being put on her by her peers? Did she walk anyway?

You have certainly been challenged to do things you were not able to do or did not want to do. You must have heard one of the following statements:

I bet you can't do it.
I dare you to do it!

How many of you fall into that trap even if it means breaking a rule, hurting yourself, or hurting someone else? That kind of pressure comes straight from your worst enemy: Satan himself.

Listen to what Satan dared Jesus to do:

— command stones to become bread
— throw himself down from the pinnacle of the temple
— fall down and worship him

Jesus could have carried out Satan's commands, but he chose not to. "Then the devil left him, and suddenly angels came and waited on him" (Matthew 4:1–11).

God gave you a conscience and a good mind. God planted a sense of right and wrong in your very being. You know if your actions are right or wrong. When someone dares you to do something that is wrong, listen to your conscience. I am pretty sure your conscience will say, "Don't do it. It's wrong. Don't fall for peer pressure."

However, in most cases, students suppress that advice. They silence their conscience. They tell their conscience to be quiet. "Don't speak!" they say.

They dismiss that advice and go ahead and do what's wrong because they want to show somebody they are daring enough to do something that is contrary to their knowledge of right and wrong.

Imagine a group of your peers saying, "I dare you to beat up so-and-so." Something inside of you replies, "If I don't do it, I will be laughed at by the others. Who wants to be laughed at? Who wants to feel small before so many friends? I'll show them that I can do it." Even though you know you really should not, you go ahead and do it to prove something.

You end up feeling worse than when you started. You feel embarrassed because you didn't do a good job. So-and-so was much bigger and stronger than you, and after the first punch, you became a coward and ran away. You couldn't beat him. All you could do was change your mind.

In the first place, you should have said, "I know who I am. I am a child of God. I don't have to prove anything to my peers."

When the Devil told Jesus to dare himself to prove that he was the Son of God, Jesus simply quoted scripture verses at him and sent him fleeing. Jesus defeated the Devil. You can do the same. Quote some scripture verses to your peers and send them fleeing. Be strong and courageous. God is with you. Say to yourself, "Greater is he that is in me than he that is in the world" (1John 4:4).

One of the best stories of courage I know of in the Bible is the story of Daniel, Shadrach, Meshach, and Abednego. You can read the story in the Book of Daniel, chapter 1:3-17 The young lads were captured in their hometown and taken to a foreign land. They were dared to give up their food and eat the food of that foreign land or face the consequences. They refused to give in to the pressure. They refused to eat the food.

On another occasion, Daniel's three friends were told to fall down and adore the king when they heard the sound of the horn, pipe, lyre, harp, drum, and the entire musical ensemble. They were to fall down and worship the golden statue that King Nebuchadnezzar had set up. They were told that whoever did not fall down and worship would immediately be thrown into a furnace of blazing fire.

They refused to give in to the pressure. Can you imagine that? They knew the consequences of their refusal, yet they went ahead and refused to worship the golden statue. They were thrown into the furnace of blazing fire. They walked around in the midst of the flames, singing hymns to God, praying to God, and blessing the Lord. The fire did not touch them at all or cause them any pain or distress.

When the king learned that they were still alive, he called them out of the fire and blessed God since he had miraculously saved them from the flames (Daniel 3:1-95). What an incredible story! The young men did not yield to the pressure from the king. How many of you have the courage to say no to somebody who tells you to do something outrageous?

If someone offers you a joint, will you refuse it? Can you say no when you know it will go against your conscience, hurt your family, be bad for your health, or hurt your God? Do you ever have to say yes to peer pressure?

Learn from Jesus—and from Daniel and his companions—not to give in to pressure. Stand up with your own principles and be brave. You will have to make a commitment to read your Bible and learn some of the verses so you have them ready to use when you are put into a dangerous situation. Jesus learned Bible verses, the Devil learned Bible verses, and I learned Bible verses. Now it's your turn to learn Bible verses too.

Sometimes the pressure comes from within. You can have intense pressure from within to quit school, start drugs, have impure thoughts, and be dishonest. Don't give in to those pressures either. Don't repeat the excuses I often hear from students:

> *Everybody is doing it.*
> *It's no big deal*
> *There's nothing wrong with that.*
> *I just want them to accept me.*
> *God understands.*
> *I'm only human.*
> *I'm not an island.*
> *Why can't I be like everybody else?*
> *It's my body. I can do what I like with it.*

Just as you can't fight fire with fire, you cannot fight thoughts with thoughts. You have to fight fire with water, and you have to fight thoughts with Bible verses. Learn enough verses so that when the pressure comes, whether it is from outside or inside, you are ready to fight. Stick to what is right, and God will see you through.

Prayer

Jesus, you resisted pressure when the Devil came to you and asked you to perform for him. You refused to change stone to bread, jump down from the pinnacle of the temple, and fall down and worship him. I would like to follow your example of using Bible verses to resist any pressure that may come from my family, my friends, or even from myself. Amen.

Princes and Princesses

When I look at your heavens,
The work of your fingers,
The moon and the stars that
You have established;
What are human beings that you
Are mindful of them,
Mortals that you care for them?
Yet you have made them a little
Lower than God,
And crowned them with glory and honour.
—Psalm 8:3–5

What a beautiful group of young people I see before me! I thank God for all young people. Every day, I see their cute faces, their pretty faces, and their handsome faces. Some of you may never have heard anyone say such nice things about you, but I am not afraid to say so. I delight in letting young people know how wonderful they are, and I know without a doubt that God sees you exactly that way. You are God's unique creation. God created the universe, the planets, the stars, the galaxies, the animals, the mountains, and humankind.

There is no one alive who can boast that he or she made the universe—not even a small part of it. Have you ever heard anyone claim to own the sun or the earth? Have you ever heard anyone say, "The moon is mine, I made it"? No! That was the work of your God. He is awesome; he is king of the universe!

If God is king, what does that make you? That makes you his prince or his princess. Yes, you are a prince or a princess, and you don't even know it. This morning, I stopped to talk to Prince Cedric, Prince Chris, Princess Sandra, Princess Keisha, and Princess Simone. And who are you? Kimberly. Try saying, "I am Princess Kimberly."

Since you are princes and princesses, you have to show dignity and integrity in your behaviour. You may have to develop new thoughts, new speech, new actions, new friendships, and a new attitude.

You belong to God's heavenly kingdom. You are royalty—just like any earthly king or queen's children. Hold your head up high. Know that you have divine royal blood running through your veins.

When you look into the mirror in the morning, say, "I am a child of God. I am royalty. I am from the royal bloodline of God. I am a prince or I am a princess, as the case might be. My Father is a king, and I know it." Leave for school with great confidence and enthusiasm. Feel good about yourself! You are going to meet other princes and princesses.

Tell yourself that you are going out into your Father's universe to enjoy the good things he has created for you, and for those with whom you will come into contact (friends and enemies). You all belong to a heavenly kingdom. You are very precious to God. He dearly loves you. Unfortunately, many young people ask me certain questions over and over again.

> *How can God love me? I am bad.*
> *Am I good?*
> *Will I go to heaven? I am bad.*
> *Can God forgive me for all the bad things I did?*

There are others who tell me that when they die, they will go to that bad place. I always have to assure them that they are good. I tell them that everyone is capable of making bad choices, but that does not make us bad persons. God is good, and what he made is good. Read the creation story in the Bible, and you will find out that after each day's work, God saw what he had made and called it good. On the sixth day, God created his finest work.

God created humankind in his image. He created them male and female (Genesis 1:27). God saw everything he had made, and he called it very good. How can you tell me that you are bad?

You cannot look at what God made and call it bad. God made you. You are God's masterpiece. You are not bad. In fact, you are very good. If young people believe they are bad because they do bad things, they should stop doing bad things immediately. If they do, they will see themselves as God sees them.

Ask God to forgive you. He will forgive you, and he will forget about it. You must receive his forgiveness, say thanks, go forward, and do what is right. You may have to develop new thoughts, new speech, new actions, new friendships, and a new attitude. This may be your time to change—so begin immediately.

In the Old Testament, God sometimes became angry with the people and showed them his wrath, but in the New Testament, Jesus caused us to see God differently. Now we see a merciful God, a loving God, a long-suffering God, a compassionate God, and a good God. Does that make you feel good about yourself now?

When God looks at you, he says, "Here is my special work of creation! I am very proud of Prince (fill in your name) or Princess (fill in your name)." God sees you as *very* good. There is not another one like you anywhere in the whole world. You are God's unique creation, good princes and princesses. Celebrate that!

Prayer

Dear Heavenly Father, thank you for making me such a special person. I praise you because I am fearfully and wonderfully made. Wonderful are your works; that I know very well (Psalm 139:14).

PGF (Put God First)

Remember your creator in the days of your
youth,
Before the days of trouble come and the years
draw near when you will say,
"I have no pleasure in them"
—Ecclesiastes 12–1

Early one morning, many years ago, I went to buy
something from a neighbourhood store. The storekeeper
had not arrived yet, so I waited outside the door.

Several minutes passed before the storekeeper
arrived. He parked his van on the lot, got out, locked
the door, and walked over to the store. He took his
key out of his pocket and unlocked the door. I was a
little impatient and had hoped to get inside, find what I
wanted quickly, pay for it, and get out. After all, I had
already wasted ten minutes while waiting to get into
the store.

God wanted to teach me something. As soon as the
storekeeper opened the door, I followed him in. What
I witnessed was strange. Instead of the storekeeper
asking me a question or opening up the cash register
to attend to me and send me on my way, he turned to a
statue on the wall and started praying. The storekeeper
did not care that I was in the store. He did not pay any
attention to me.

He continued praying, and I had to wait until he had finished. I said to myself, "This storekeeper has put God first. Could I have done that?" At the time, my answer would have been no. Instead, I coined the phrase: *Put God first.*

I really think God wanted me to learn from that person, which is why he brought me to that particular store early in the morning on that day. I did learn the lesson. I did learn to put God first.

As if God felt that I hadn't learned the lesson well enough, he put me in another situation in another store. I went into a store to look for a gift for my baby nephew. The first thing I noticed was that nobody was in the store. I thought, *I can take the whole store away. There's no one here.*

I walked around and looked for that special gift. Lo and behold, I found the storekeeper. He was praying in the back of the store. I said to God, "Not again. I got your message the first time. I know you want me to spend more time with you. Okay, you've got it. I will spend more time praying to you. I will put you first."

What about you? Do you put God first? When you wake in the morning, is your first thought about God? Do you say, "Thank you, God, for this fresh new day?" When you do something wrong, is your first thought about God? Do you say, "I am sorry, Lord. Please forgive me"?

How many of you believe that you are only allowed to pray in church once a week? Do you know that you can put God first in your games on the playground?

Perhaps if you did, there would be less bullying, selfishness, arguments, being mean to one another, and rejection. There could be more kindness, sharing, caring, gentleness, inclusion, and love.

You can put God first before you eat your meals. You can put God first when you enter your school bus. You can find many times during the day to speak to God first. After all, what is prayer? Prayer is having a conversation with God.

Are you ashamed of praying in public? Do you only pray when you are alone? Are you like that storekeeper in my story and pray even though you know there is someone around? Do you ask God to wait? Are you ashamed to put God first when you are having a meal in public? Are you ashamed to say grace over that meal before you eat it? Do you have to look around to see if others are watching? If they are, would you be ashamed and not put God first?

Prayer

Dear God, you are special to me. I want to put you first in all I do and say. Give me the courage to be brave enough to spend more time with you each day. Amen.

Rules for the New Life

So then, putting away falsehood, let all of us
speak the truth to our neighbours,
For we are members of one another. Be angry,
but do not sin.
Do not let the sun go down on your anger, and
do not make room for the devil.
Therefore, be imitators of God as beloved
children, and live in love,
As Christ loved us and gave himself up for us,
A fragrant offering and sacrifice to God.
—Ephesians 4:25–27, 5:1–2

How many of you like new things—new shoes, new
sweaters, new books, new video games, new bicycles,
and new foods?

As a very young girl, I attended the primary school
in my village. I was always very happy to attend school
until one day I suffered a great disappointment. I wanted
a new pair of shoes; the pair I was wearing had holes
in the soles. I showed them to my mom and asked if I
could get a new pair of shoes. She said that she could not
afford to buy me a new pair of shoes then, but I could
wear my brother's old shoes. I was devastated!

*Imagine going to school wearing my brother's old
shoes! No way! I am a girl. All the children in school
would laugh at me.* I was totally ashamed. I preferred to
wear my old shoes with the holes in the soles.

In those days, children were not allowed to question their parents. What they said was what the children did. I could not argue, talk back, defend myself, or make a suggestion. I had to obey without questioning. All I could do was cry and cry and cry. When all the crying was over, I wiped the tears from my eyes, put on my brother's old shoes and left for school. When I reached the school, I began to cry all over again. My friends saw me crying and asked me why I was crying. I told them my story, and as you would expect, the children taunted me for wearing my brother's old shoes. I wanted new shoes, but I got old shoes.

The Apostle Paul wrote to the people of Ephesus about rules for the new life. In the letter, Paul calls on the Ephesians to make a new start. Paul gave them a new set of rules. We can learn these lessons and start putting them into practice immediately.

> *Speak the truth to our neighbours.*
> *Be kind and loving to all.*
> *Treat others with respect.*
> *Do not seek revenge.*

Be angry but do not sin. It is all right to become angry. Anger is an emotion that each one of us has. All of us express that emotion at some time or another. Some of us become angrier than others, but we all use our anger.

Paul says we should not commit sin while we are angry. If someone bears false witness against you,

you might want to show anger toward that person. That's okay, but do not turn around and stomp on that person's big toe or call the person a ridiculous name. Do not become violent during your arguments or misunderstandings.

Who believes that these rules are easy to keep? I think they are rather difficult to keep, but with God's help, we can become winners. The key is to keep practicing them on a daily basis. We will create harmony in our communities.

God wants all of us to live in love, and he gives us many opportunities everyday to show others the love that is within us. Let us show one another that we are serious about following Paul's new rules for our lives.

Prayer

Lord Jesus, give me the courage to grow in this new life. Lead me to choose to do what is right in your sight. Amen.

Service to God and People

Jesus, knowing that the Father had given all
things into his hands,
And that he had come from God and was going
to God,
Got up from the table, took off his outer robe,
And tied a towel around himself.
Then he poured water into a basin and began to
wash the disciples' feet
And to wipe them with the towel that was tied
around him.
—John 13:3–5

When God wanted to choose a mother for his Son, he
chose Mary. He knew that Mary would be a willing
servant, but he had to offer the position to her and let
her choose. He sent Archangel Gabriel to ask her.

She said, "Behold the handmaid of the Lord, be it
done unto me according to thy word." In other words,
Mary said, "I am your servant, and I am willing to do
whatever you ask me to do."

God was certainly pleased with Mary's willingness
to serve. Because she said, "Yes, I will serve," she
became the mother of Jesus. What an honour for Mary!
Are we as willing as Mary was to serve God when he
calls upon us? We cannot truly serve God unless we are
willing to serve those around us.

Jesus said, "Whatever you do to the least of my brethren, you do to me."

Serving other people is just like serving God; therefore, all of us should welcome opportunities to serve willingly.

We can serve them in our homes, schools, churches, and communities. We can serve our country too—as police officers, soldiers, or firefighters. If your teacher asks you to clean the chalkboard, and you do that service willingly, you serve your teacher and your classmates— and you serve God. You can feel happy because you have answered the call to serve.

Every day, you should be on the lookout for opportunities to serve. If you look, you will find. God will send you many opportunities. Take advantage of them, knowing that God is noticing what you are doing. In the end, he will look at you and say, "Well done, my good and faithful servant!"

On the night he was betrayed, Jesus showed us how to serve when he took a towel, wrapped it around his waist, and washed his disciples' feet (John 13:3–5). Afterward, he said, "If I, your Lord and teacher, have washed your feet, you also ought to wash one another's feet. For I have set you an example that you should do as I have done to you" (John 13:14–15).

There are so many opportunities for you to imitate your Lord and serve others. You can help your classmates who are in wheelchairs. They are eager to go out and play just like you. Help them get out safely. When you notice other students feeling sad or lonely, give a helping hand, say a kind word to them, and help them if they need it. You can serve in soup kitchens or at food banks in your community. There are numerous ways for all of us to serve God and other people.

Do not get into the habit of only serving outside your home. Form the habit of serving those in your own family too. That is where your service should begin. Begin with those closest to you. Then you can reach out to those in your school community, your church community, your city, your country, and the world.

You learn to serve by serving those in your own household. If your mom is tired, help her. If your dad is tired, offer to help him. Continue bringing food for the food banks. Volunteer to help those in need. There are so many opportunities for you to serve others. You cannot truly say, "I have no one to serve."

Jesus said he did not come into this world to be served. He came to serve. Service is part of the reason why God made you, so you should be happy to serve God and people. Until you can fulfill God's purpose for your life, you will wander and not see the purpose for being here on earth. Good deeds are your service! Here are a few lines of a song I wrote:

Stressed out? Find somebody to serve.
Angry? Find some cause to serve.
No! No! No! Serving yourself is not the answer.
It gets you more of what you do not want.
The good Lord Jesus said, "I came to serve—
not to be served" (Mark 10:45).

Saying, "Let me serve you" is far better than "Let me serve me."

Prayer

Dear God, open my eyes so that I can see you in my neighbours and be willing to serve them all the days of my life. Amen

Shake It Off

I write to you young people, because you are
strong and the Word of God abides in you,
and you have overcome the evil one.
—I John 2:14

Once upon a time, a farmer had a donkey. It was a good, strong, useful donkey. Best of all, it was a hardworking donkey. Every second day, it hauled the farmer's crops to the market. Life on the farm was fine for the donkey. It was fed three times a day. It was groomed once a week, and it was given a treat twice a day. How about that for good treatment?

When the donkey became old and useless, it could no longer work for the farmer. The farmer became very disappointed with the donkey, dug a pit in his backyard, and threw the old donkey in the hole. The donkey stood in the pit, not knowing what to do.

In the mornings and evenings, the farmer would rake up the dead leaves, twigs, old papers, and every kind of trash. He would dump it on the donkey in the pit.

The donkey was old and weak and useless, but it was not foolish. When the farmer threw the trash on it, the donkey would shake it off, trample it under its feet, and raise itself on the trash. This went on for days. Eventually, the donkey raised himself up high above the pit, walked out of there, and escaped down the road.

There is some similarity between the story of the donkey and the story of the Apostle Paul (Acts 28:1–6). On a cold, rainy day, Paul gathered a bundle of brushwood out it in a fire. The heat drove out a viper. It fastened itself on Paul's hand and would have killed him. Those who saw what happened expected Paul to swell up or drop dead, but Paul shook the creature into the fire and suffered no harm—just like the donkey shook off the trash and suffered no harm.

You too can shake off trash talk and suffer no harm. Do you know persons who dump trash on you day after day? Learn a lesson from Paul and the donkey. Shake it off!

You will encounter three kinds of people who throw trash in your life.

Family and relatives
Friends, enemies, and other people
Yourself

Family and Relatives

You can't do it. Don't even try it.
You are useless. Why were you born anyway?
You'll never amount to anything good.
You are no good. You are good for nothing.
You give me so much trouble.
Who do you think you are? There is no one in our family or among our relatives who is a doctor, a lawyer, or a teacher! Why do you

think you can become a doctor, a lawyer, or a
teacher? Who said you have the brains for such
jobs?

Friends, Enemies, and Other People

You're too short.
You're too tall.
You're too fat.
You're too skinny.
You're bad.
You are of the Devil.
You're so slow.
You will never get it.
Who do you think you are?
What makes you think you are so special?
You're a geek (wimp, idiot, banana head, or
moron).

How should you respond when you hear such remarks pronounced over you? Shake them off! Don't receive their trash. Refuse to accept their trash, and it will go right back to them.

If Paul and the donkey could do it, then you can too. Shake it off! Trample it under your feet and move on. Say to yourself, "I am a child of God. I am made in the image of God. I am able to do all things through Christ who strengthens me" (Philippians 4:13).

Remember that God loves you—even when it seems like no one else does.

Yourself

> *I can't do anything right. I'm not like James or Mae. They know everything, and I know nothing.*
> *I always get everything wrong. I am no good. I am a banana head.*
> *I am brain dead. I hate my life. Why was I born? I am a dummy. I am so silly. I am really stupid. If only I had a longer nose, blue eyes, shorter limbs, or longer limbs.*
> *I do not think I can make it in this world.*
> *I'm not that popular in school. I have no friends. Nobody likes me. People don't want me on their teams. No one ever gives me a chance. I feel so depressed.*
> *I feel sick to my stomach. This headache will never leave me. It comes back every Monday morning.*
> *I feel my heart is giving out. I feel like I am going to die.*
> *I can't be all that I want to be. I am too sickly. I am a loser.*
> *My life is really messed up. I am really bad. I have a Devil in me, and I am so discouraged.*

Watch what you say to yourself! Don't dump trash on yourself. It is bad enough that other persons dump trash on you, but it is worse when you dump trash on yourself. See yourself as you really are. You are a child of God. You are wonderfully made. You are princes and princesses. You belong to God's royal family. Your Father, God, is a king.

He is king of all kings, and you are his precious sons and daughters. Celebrate that! Hold your head up high! Believe in yourself! You are here on earth to fulfill a purpose in your life. Do not go through life being angry about the trash that others (and you) dump on you. If you discover your purpose for being alive and work at it consistently, you will achieve it. Shake off the trash, trample it under your feet, and move on.

Now stand up tall and practice our response to trash throwers:

> *Shake it off! (Everyone, shake your shoulders from side to side, and up and down.)*
> *Trample it under your feet! (Everyone, lift your feet up, one at a time, and bring them down on the trash.)*
> *Raise yourself high up! (Everyone, lift yourself up on your toes and move ahead one step.)*

Good! Now you know what to do when someone throws trash on you and you do not like it. Don't get mad. Don't be afraid. Shake it off! Trample it under your feet and move on.

Stop! Reflect on what you are saying over yourself, your family, your friends, and your enemies.

Prayer

My God, I know that I am wonderfully made. I am made in your image and likeness. Help me never to forget this. Amen.

Spiritual Makeover

My soul is satisfied as with a rich feast,
And my mouth praises you with joyful lips
When I think of you on my bed,
And meditate on you in the
Watches of the night;
For you have been my help,
And in the shadow of your wings,
I sing for joy.
—Psalm 63:5–7

How many of you heard the story of the Pentecost? The Holy Spirit came down to the apostles. The Holy Spirit gave them the ability to speak in other languages. The apostles were amazed and perplexed.

"What does this mean? But others sneered and said, 'They are filled with new wine'" (Acts of the Apostles 2:1–12).

People thought they were drunk from too much alcohol. Did you know that people can become drunk with the Holy Spirit too?

The Holy Spirit changed the apostles' lives forever. Before Pentecost, the apostles were weak, scared, timid persons. They hid out in an upper room in Jerusalem because Jesus had left them and returned to heaven. Nine days later, the Holy Spirit descended upon them and gave them the boldness and courage they lacked.

They were ready to go into the world and proclaim the good news to creation (Mark 16:15).

Peter went out to the crowd that had gathered in Jerusalem for Pentecost and gave his first sermon. He exclaimed, "Men of Judea and all who live in Jerusalem, let this be known to you. Listen to what I say. Indeed these are not drunk as you suppose, for it is only nine o'clock in the morning" (Acts 2:14–15). And with great boldness, he preached his first sermon.

In my native land, I would sometimes see intoxicated people walking along the streets. They did not have to tell me they drank too much alcohol because their actions spoke to me. They were swaying and staggering. Their hands were swinging in the air, their feet were flailing, they were swearing, and they were dribbling. I knew they were drunk from too much alcohol. From a person's actions, you can usually determine what they are up to.

In the same way, I can find a good indication of whether a person is filled with the Holy Spirit or not. Their words and actions are telltale signs. How do they treat one another? Are they kind and polite? Do they forgive others for hurting them? Do kind words come out of their mouths? Are they patient with one another? Do they share when they can? Do they help one another understand difficult things? Do they treat one another as brothers and sisters in Christ? Do they show love? Are they peacemakers?

If many of the above actions are visible in a person, there is a good sign the person is full of the Holy

Spirit. One can say that that person is drunk with the Holy Spirit as the apostles were thought to be during Pentecost.

I came across a group of children playing outside. From the moment I laid eyes on them, I could sense a spirit of division and animosity (left out and dislike). One girl was the target of the division and animosity. No one was playing with her, no one was speaking to her, and no one asked her to come join in the fun. As a matter of fact, a sarcastic remark was hurled at her. Someone said, "You can't play with us."

I felt as though she was under an attack. The atmosphere was so tense. I looked at the situation as I always do when I come across a situation that needs my attention. I tried to find the cause for the division and animosity. I spent a moment observing the behaviour of the children, and I thought, *these actions do not prove to me that these children have the Holy Spirit in them.*

Actions speak louder than words. The children did not have to tell me anything. Their actions told me everything I wanted to know about the situation.

I said, "The Holy Spirit is in this group now. Who can believe that?"

Everybody looked up at me in silence and waited for my next words.

I said, "I sense there is some misunderstanding among you kids."

"We don't like her. She is not our friend," said one child.

I replied, "I can see that, but now you must give way to the Holy Spirit that is within you and in this group.

The Holy Spirit is your comforter. The Holy Spirit is your helper. The Holy Spirit helps you understand things that might be difficult to understand. We all carry the gifts of the Holy Spirit. What are the gifts of the Holy Spirit? They are love, joy, peace, patience, kindness, generosity, faithfulness, gentleness, and self-control (Galatians 5:22–23).

Everyone in the group reached out to the girl, and the entire atmosphere in that group changed.

I said, "Jesus said, 'Love one another as I have loved you'" (John 13: 34). What do you not understand from that advice? In this group, you are all brothers and sisters in Christ. Jesus died for each and every one of you. You have to show love, a tender heart, and patience to all your brothers and sisters. God does not have favourites. He loves us all the same."

A child got up, took the girl's hand, and brought her closer to the group.

I said, "That is a beautiful gesture. Why did you bring her nearer to the group?"

The boy said, "I heard what you said about the Holy Spirit, and I decided to be kind to her. I invited her to join us."

I replied, "Beautiful!"

Another child asked, "Do you want to play?"

The girl replied, "Yes!"

I was totally amazed. I didn't expect to see that reaction from the group.

Another child said, "Sorry. We want to be your friend."

Other students got up and said, "Sorry. We want to be your friends."

I was so overwhelmed that I could not say anything else. After the game was over, the children departed—with the girl. She had become the centre of the group.

I followed, praising and glorifying God for what was accomplished that day. I said, "Thank you, Holy Spirit. Thanks for your power."

You can certainly learn something from this story. The children showed me that even if I cannot reach them, the Holy Spirit can. How about your life? Are you drunk with the Holy Spirit? Can the Holy Spirit change you too? What can you do to show that the Holy Spirit is working within you?

Prayer

Holy Spirit, help us remember that we are brothers and sisters in Christ. When one brother or sister hurts, we all hurt. Give us the words to console each person going through any kind of physical, emotional, or mental pain. Give us true love for one another. We know you love us. Help us love all our friends as Jesus loved his disciples and apostles. We want to be strong in the Lord. Amen.

The Goodness of God

Trust in him at all times,
O people;
Pour out your heart before him;
God is a refuge for us.
—Psalm 62:8

How many of you have asked God for something and did not get it? You may have felt badly about it and never wanted to talk to God anymore. Earlier, we established the fact that God is good. If we ask him for something that is not good for us, should God withhold it from us? Yes, he should. We should be thankful that he did so. Listen to these two stories to see what I mean.

A mother was sitting at table with her toddler on her lap. The toddler looked up and saw a shiny, sharp knife on the table. She asked for it, cried, and pointed to the knife. The mom refused to give it to her, but the toddler insisted on having it. She even began to cry and throw a tantrum. Would she be a good mom if she gave the toddler the knife because she asked for it? Of course not.

Should the Heavenly Father give you something bad because you asked for it? Think about it! Trust God to give you good things. Scripture says that even evil people know how to give good gifts to their children (Matthew 7:11).Why should the Heavenly Father give you bad gifts simply because you asked for them? You should say, "I did not get what I asked for because God knows it is bad for me. I trust him to do what is right for me. Thank you, God."

In the days when the hula hoop was fashionable, a five-year-old boy asked his mother to buy him one. She said no, but he persisted. "All my friends have hula hoops. Why can't I get one?"

His mother got tired of his pleadings and decided to make him one. She took a reed, bent it into a circle, and tied the two ends together with some string. When she gave it to her son, he was excited. It was not the real thing, but at last he had something to put around his waist and twist. He did this for a few days and was quite happy.

When he twisted one day, the string came loose, the ends separated, and one end struck him in the eye. His mother was so sorry that she gave in to his pleading and allowed him to have a hula hoop. She blamed herself for her son's misfortune.

It is the same way with the Heavenly Father. He would feel sorry too if he gave us something that was not good for us. Here is the best attitude to adopt when we pray for something: If you get it, thank your Heavenly Father. If you do not get it, thank your Heavenly Father as well.

This is the best way to deal with our petition prayers. A petition is when we ask for something. Stop blaming God! God is interested in our welfare. The mistake we make is to compare ourselves with others. Do not compare your answers with somebody else's answer, because what might be good for that person might not be good for you. Do not want another person's answered prayer for yourself. Get what is good for you.

You have a test coming up soon. Your teacher told you to study, your parents told you to study, and your best friend told you to study. You think, *I do not need to study. I will do well. It will be a piece of cake.*

You enter the test room, turn over your paper, and read the questions. To your amazement, you discover that you do not have a clue about how or where to begin. You cannot figure out any of the answers.

At this time, a wild thought comes into your mind: *I'll pray and ask God to help me.* You mumble some prayers and think God will take care of the matter.

I'm sorry to say that God is not a magician. In spite of your prayers, you did very poorly on the test. You are disappointed because God did not help you. What do you do? You blame God for your failure when you should be blaming yourself for not heeding the advice of your teacher, your parents, and your best friend. You could not do the work because you did not study. That is it! Plain and simple! God had nothing to do with you failing the test.

However, do not be discouraged. Keep on praying! Keep on making your requests known to God. God always answers our prayers. He might not answer exactly as we want him to, but he does answer us. He might give us something better than what we asked for. That has happened to me on several occasions. He might answer your prayers immediately.

An answer is always given in one of three ways:

No. I have something better for you.
Yes.
Not now—later.

God has our best interests at heart, and he does answer us. God hears us the very first time we pray. Remember that God is not a magician. Abracadabra does not work with God.

Learn from Jesus. He prayed three times for God to stop the Crucifixion, but he also said, "Not my will, but yours be done" (Luke 22:42). The following day, he went through with the Crucifixion.

Jesus only wanted to do what God wanted him to do. We should follow Jesus' example. Repeat, "Not my will, but God's will be done." In other words, it is not what I want—it is what God wants for me.

Prayer

Thank you, Lord. You always answer my prayers in the way that is best for me. At the end of my petitions to you, help me remember to say, "Not my will, but your will be done." Amen.

The Presence of God

But for me it is good to be near God;
I have made the Lord God my refuge,
To tell of all your works.
—Psalm 73:28

On one occasion I conducted an experiment with my students to help them understand the presence of God. I began by asking a simple question, "How many of you believe that this room is full of air?" Next I said, "Look up! Look down! Look under your desk! Look all around you! Can you see the air in this room?" No one answered the question, so I continued. "I am going to perform an experiment to show you that even though you cannot see the air in this room, there is an abundance of air in here." Everyone was as quiet as mice, and very attentive.

I continued, "I will use this large clear garbage bag to conduct my experiment. See the bag! It is folded. It is very flat. It has nothing inside of it. Now, I will unfold it. Look carefully. Do not take your eyes off the bag. See! There is still nothing in it. Now, I will open the mouth and go around the room and catch the air that we cannot see. Look carefully! I will start here, in front of the room, and then I will go down this side, then to the back of the room, and down the middle. I will lift the bag up to the ceiling. Why is the bag becoming bigger and bigger? There must be an abundance of something in the bag. I am closing the mouth of the bag. Look at the bag now! It is full of something. I will pass it around for you to feel it or give it a punch.

Now I am going to let out what is inside the bag. Look very carefully to see what comes out. I am now opening the mouth of the bag very slowly, and letting what is inside the bag escape. Are you ready? Okay. One, two, three. Poof! Did you see the thing escape? What was it, and where did it go?" One student answered, "Air, and it went back in the room." I replied, "Good answers! The bag was full of the air I captured from inside the room. Magic, you say? No, it is not. The air was there all along. Now, I do not think that anyone will dare to say, "There is no such thing as air! If there is I would see it!"

How many of you believe God is in this room? Let's presume that everyone believes that God is here right now, can you see him? If you cannot see him, does that mean he is not here? Can you see why I did the experiment with the bag and the air? God is here, right here in this room. He is also in you and in me. Your body is the temple of God. Did you know that? Yes, God the Father, the Son, and the Holy Spirit live in you. Scripture says, 'Greater is he (God) that is in you, than he that is in the world' (1 John 4:4).

"God is everywhere. He is on the bus you ride to school. He is in the car that brings you to church. He is on the playground. He is in the mall. He is in your house. He is in the sports arena. He is everywhere—just like air is everywhere."

Never say, "Since I cannot see him, I cannot believe he is here." As a matter of fact, you should not want to see God now.

I was driving down a street and had difficulty seeing the road ahead of me. The bright sun affected my vision. I closed my eyes for a second, because I could not look at the sun. I pulled down the visor to protect my eyes from the glare, and I thought to myself, *if I cannot look at the sun, how can I look at God? He must be a trillion times brighter than the sun.* Believe me when I say I do not want to see God now.

Did you hear what happened to Moses after he came back from a visit with God? The people could not look at Moses. Some of God's splendour had rubbed off on Moses, and his face shone so brightly that people could not look at him. Moses had to wear a veil over his face whenever he wanted to speak to the people (Exodus 34:29). Can you imagine that? Do you want to see God now? You will have plenty of time to see God after you die. You will have an eternity to see him. While you are here on earth, all God wants you to do is believe in your heart that he exists, and that he is present right here with you and with me.

I had another experience. One day on my way home from work, I was almost thrown off the sidewalk by a huge gust of wind. The wind hit my face very violently. When I recovered from the blast, I thought about the experience. I thought, *God is like the wind. I did not see the wind, but I cannot say the wind was not there.*

I began thinking about other things that I cannot see, but I know exist. Have you ever seen gravity? Because you have never seen it, can you say it does not exist?

Someone told me that I have a spleen. I have never seen it, but can I say that it is not there because I have never seen it? It is the same with the presence of God. We cannot see him, but he is very close to us. After my experience with that violent wind on my way home from work, the presence of God took on a deeper meaning for me. I do not have to see God to know he exists. With all my heart, I believe he is.

Prayer

My God, I believe you are present everywhere. I adore you, I praise you, I thank you, and I love you. Amen.

Work Out Your Choices

Therefore prepare your minds for action; discipline yourselves,
Set all your hope on the grace that Jesus Christ will bring you when he is revealed. Like obedient children, do not be conformed
To the desires that you formerly had in ignorance. Instead, as he who called you is holy, be holy yourselves in all your conduct;
For it is written, "You shall be holy, for I am holy."
—1 Peter 1:13–16

Do you know that you make thousands of choices on a daily basis? Some of those choices are good choices, and some of them are bad choices. Some are the right choices, and some are the wrong choices. What kinds of choices are you going to make today? Think about it!

I hope you are going to make good choices. I hope you are going to make the right choices. Our habits determine our choices. Habits are things we have been doing for such a long time that they have become automatic actions. We get up every morning and thank God for the gift of a new day. That is a habit. We do it without thinking about it.

Choices come out of our habits. Some of us have a habit of being rude, harsh, obnoxious, or bullying. When we are faced with a situation, how will we respond?

We can choose to respond in a rude, harsh, obnoxious fashion—or like a bully. What would your choice be?

Some of us have a habit of being pleasant, kind, loving, forgiving, peaceful, and gentle. When we are faced with a situation, how will we respond? We can choose to respond in a pleasant, kind, respectful, peaceful, helpful, and gentle fashion. What would your choice be?

The children of Israel chose to become rebellious and turned away from loving and serving the one true God. Joshua, their leader, said, "Choose this day whom you may serve.... But as for me and my household, we will serve the Lord" (Joshua 24:15). Joshua made a choice, a very good choice, indeed. No doubt his choice brought him great blessings from God.

You can make choices that could change your life. You can choose to be lazy or you can choose to be industrious which means hard-working. Both of these are our own choices. Which will you choose?

Do you get annoyed very quickly? Does it annoy you when someone, who is sitting right behind you, begins tapping on his or her desk? Would you get up, go over to the person, and show your anger? What better choice could you make?

Some persons have the habit of swearing or using profane language. If a friend brings that to your attention, are you going to make the choice to curb your tongue, or mistreat your friend? Again, it's your choice, but I would say to you, "Don't let your choices, good ones or bad ones, take control of you. Strive to do what is right.

God will give you the ability to make the right choices. In an unpleasant situation, you can make the choice to turn around and go in the opposite direction. Don't be afraid to call on God for help when you need it. Some choices are difficult, especially when the choice looks good. Deep in your spirit, you know it's bad and it could lead you into trouble. What happens when you realize you made the wrong choice?

In today's society, bullying has become a way of life for some people. Bullying is never the right choice; it is always the wrong choice. You could hurt yourself or those around you—even your best friends. To be a bully is really not cool at all. We can always find ways to settle our differences if we follow Jesus' plan.

Have you ever wondered why some kids bully others? I did, and one of the reasons I came up with is that someone else bullied them. *Since I was bullied, I will bully too.* They learned the pattern of bullying from someone else. Is that a good reason for bullying? Of course not! You have the ability to make choices. You can choose not to continue the cycle of bullying.

You can say, "Bullying stops with me."

I do not think anyone is born a bully—or born to be a bully. Bullies are selfish. They have to have everything their way. If they don't, they resort to bullying to get their way.

When you make the wrong choice, don't just stay there and feel sorry for yourself. Get up and make the change. Continue in a new direction. Learn a lesson from your wrong choice and make sure the lesson teaches you to make better choices in the future. We learn from the choices we make.

I made a bad choice after I had been teaching for twenty years. I made the choice to quit teaching and become an office secretary. I took a crash course in secretarial procedures, but after graduation, I could not find a job. No one would hire me.

Just as I was about to become discouraged, I received a telephone call. The caller offered me a job in teaching. I accepted the teaching job. Do you think I made the right choice or the wrong choice? Without a doubt, I know I made the right choice. Teaching is my gift, and even though I wandered off the right track for some time, I turned around and got back on the right road.

When you realize you have made the wrong choice, you can make the right choice by turning around and going in the opposite direction,

It could be choosing between drugs or a drug-free life, telling lies or telling the truth, being rude or being polite, or being selfish or being selfless. The choice is yours! Work out your choices with God's help! You can do the right thing. Don't be afraid!

Prayer

Teach me your ways, Jesus. Give me the wisdom to make good choices. Amen.

Your Name Is Precious

> God appeared to Jacob again when he came
> from Paddan-aram,
> And he blessed him. God said to him, "Your
> name is Jacob;
> No longer shall you be called Jacob, but Israel
> shall be your name."
> So he was called Israel.
> —Genesis 35:9–10

How many of you believe that your name is precious? Your name is precious to God. He knows you by your name. God knows more about you than you know about yourself. How many hairs do you have on your head? I am sure you do not know, but God knows. He has every hair on your head counted (Matthew 10:30).

What are you thinking about right now? I do not know what you are thinking about, but God knows. He knows even your most secret thoughts. He knows what you will be thinking about before you think about it. That is how personal God is to you! He knew you by name even before you were born.

Let me tell you how important a name is. On the first Easter morning, Mary Magdalene went to the tomb to look for Jesus. She saw two angels who asked her why she was weeping. She answered, "They have taken away my Lord, and I do not know where they have laid him." When she had said this, she turned around and saw Jesus standing there, but she did not know it was Jesus.

Mary was actually speaking to Jesus, but she did not know it. However, when Jesus called her by her name, she recognized him immediately. That's the power of a name. She responded by calling him "Teacher." You can read the full story in (John 20: 1-16) There was no mistake about who was who. She was Mary and he was "Teacher.

Your name is very powerful too. You should never be ashamed of your name. Before I came in here, I made a list of some of your special names in my notebook. I am going to call out your names. When you hear your name, I want you to answer very boldly. Say it with conviction. *I am here. Here I am. That's my name. I like it. It sounds good. It's precious to me, and it's precious to God.*

I know that friends or bullies sometimes make fun of people's name. That hurts. Your name is precious, and everyone else's name is precious. From now on, you should make a resolution not to use false names or make fun of names.

If someone calls you a false name, do not be afraid to say, "That is not my name. You are hurting my feelings! Please use my correct name. My name is _____."

For me, God's name is precious too. Many years ago, I called on the precious name of God, and he saved me from great trouble. It happened in a series of dreams.

In the first dream, I was walking through a very large field. I was going from one village to another. While on the journey, I became aware that someone was following me.

As you would expect, that scared me. I began walking faster, and the person behind me began walking faster too. I knew the person's intention was to hurt me in some way. I became petrified (frightened to death) and screamed the only name that came to my mind. I screamed God's name. The person vanished, and I woke up from my dream. I was greatly relieved. Even though it was a dream, I thanked God for saving me.

About three months after the first dream, I had another one. I was leaving my house, and I saw someone standing outside my door. He had a harsh, cruel look on his face, and he almost scared me to death. I panicked. I could see the person's intention was to hurt me in some way. I screamed, "God," and the person vanished. I woke up and thanked God with a grateful heart. From my dreams, I discovered there was safety and protection in God's name.

In my third dream, I was driving and came up to a stop sign. I stopped. I looked in my mirror and noticed four persons coming towards my car. They were holding sticks in their hands. They scared me. I was petrified. I knew they intended to harm me. I dealt with the situation in the same way as the other two situations. I was getting used to using God's name in dangerous situations.

I looked at them and screamed, "God!"

All four of them slunk away and crossed the road. I continued my journey. I woke up and thanked God for saving me.

In the fourth dream, I was at work when a gang of thugs came up to rob me. As usual, I was petrified. I started sweating, but I kept my cool. I knew what to do.

I shouted, "God!"

However, the gang of thugs did not vanish. They were in a trance and chanted, "God! God! God! God! God!" They continued chanting God's name for a long while.

I was astonished.

As they continued chanting, their expressions moved from seriousness to repentance to sorrow to respect to holiness. I was greatly moved. I woke up and thanked God for saving me. I also thanked him for saving the gang.

The dreams caused my faith in the name of God to skyrocket. I use it all the time. I use it in every opportunity that presents itself—in letters, e-mails, and conversations.

Jesus' name is also precious. Since the Bible says that his name is above all other names, get into the habit of using his name in your prayer life.

Prayer

My name means a lot to me. Jesus, I know that you know me by name. Thank you for calling me by my own precious name. Your name is precious, too, dear Jesus. Help me never to use your name carelessly. Amen.

Review

You may choose to perform this exercise by yourself or in a group. Either way, I hope you will find it rewarding. It should increase your faith and confidence in God and in yourself.

1. How do you intend to spend this new day?

2. What is a good blessing you could say over your life?

3   As an ambassador for heaven, name one important book you will have to study to gain the knowledge you will need.

4. God showed his love for us by giving us his Son. Jesus came to earth to die for our sins. Does God stop loving us because we do wrong things?

5. Who played the first Blame Game on earth?

6. Which of these statements is true?
    a. Fear of the Lord means to be scared of God
    b. Fear of the Lord means to show respect and reverence to God.

7. Have you made any changes in your life lately? Describe the change. How has it made your life better?

8. Describe three characteristics of the God kind of love.

9. Share a personal and memorable occasion from your childhood.

10. Write a love letter to Jesus.

11. Have you discovered your gift yet? What actions are you taking to develop it?
    How do you intend to use your gift to serve others?

12. Sometimes it's really hard to make time for Jesus during the day. What can you give up to make room for a timeout with Jesus?

13. "Father, forgive them for they know not what they do." Who said this? Who is he or she referring to?

14. When was the last time someone dared you to do something you did not want to do? How did you respond to that request?

15. Circle the words that describe you:
    Special Cruel Wonderful Prince Princess Good for-Nothing Brave Good

16. Some children think the church is the only place they can meet with God. Is this true? Explain your answer.

17. Reread the five rules for the new life. What is one more rule you think would be appropriate?

18. How can you serve your country?

19. Who shook off a deadly creature from his arm? Jesus, Rebecca, or Paul?
    What creature was it?

20. Name two deeds you can do to show that the Holy Spirit is guiding you.

21. If you believe God is good and has your best interests at heart, how would you react when something you asked for did not come through for you? Would you be gracious and thank him or be mad at him?

22. Have you ever experienced the presence of God in your life? Relate your experience.

23. Can you remember when you made a good change and felt happy about it? How did that change affect your life?

24. How hurt are you when someone makes fun of your precious name? Circle the correct answer.
    Not at All   A Little   Very Hurt   Angry

Claudette Francis
4-170 Brickworks Lane, Toronto, Ontario,
Canada M6N 5H7
Cell: 647 884 4674
Email: claudettefrncs@yahoo.ca